CENTERED

Kristie Peavy

authorHOUSE®

AuthorHouse™
1663 Liberty Drive
Bloomington, IN 47403
www.authorhouse.com
Phone: 1-800-839-8640

First published by AuthorHouse   03/04/2011

ISBN: 978-1-4567-5072-5 (sc)
ISBN: 978-1-4567-5073-2 (e)

Library of Congress Control Number: 2011903592

Printed in the United States of America

Any people depicted in stock imagery provided by Thinkstock are models, and such images are being used for illustrative purposes only. Certain stock imagery © Thinkstock.

This book is printed on acid-free paper.

the miles behind me, I realize there are still many more miles
iction is simply kept at bay during the time of treatment. For
have been to treatment centers, I believe the battle is so much
lt when you leave treatment. There is an umbrella of protection
tment facility. However, you must not take the situation lightly.
o not work the steps, you most likely will not acquire the tools
survive the process.

many terrible things happen in situations where the addict
ve the serious nature of the problem. I've seen acquaintances
using or drinking, which is a direct result of not working the
lives. Hopefully, my story can help someone out there break
simplifying the steps to layman's terms.

age is that it is through soul transformation that we find
addiction. We simply use the Twelve Steps as a resource. For
e are scripture references that relate to the step. The working
reaks down who we were (dysfunctional) and reconstructs
ve become (functional). When I began working the steps,
Bible, as well. I used many AA resources, including the
All these resources together helped me find my way out of
nd into the light. Just as Matthew 17:20 promises, I was
ver my addiction, even though I had no faith in myself. I
st faith in God, and that's all He needed me to have to find

ading this book because you are a friend or loved one of
e my memoir will help you to understand what is going
of the addict. You see, we are all very much alike in the
life, yet we can be so different, as we come from different
some, the process is just easier than it may be for others.
what the addiction was, how long the person was in
d how much the person really wants to transform his or
cases, there is great shame in being an addict. In other
the only life the addict has ever known. My advice to
o whatever it takes to help that friend or loved one step
on. Each process is different. So, hang in there. Don't

This book is dedicated to Mary Ellen, for without her help, I wouldn't be
here today.

I believe there are truly angels among us who work tirelessly to make
lasting contributions to society and throw out lifelines to lost souls just
trying to find their way.

I'm keeping my promise to you.

FOREW

Matthew 17:20 ..."for truly I say u
must
You will say to this mountain, 'T
tran
Nothing will b

This book is for all those
autobiography, but a memoir
program. In each chapter, I wi
related to my life at the time. I
for both the addict and anyon
recovery process. All informati
to my personal journey. This i
the steps, and how I worked
inspiration and help to others

I would like to acknowle
as I worked through all my
appreciation to those who d
chose to embrace me, educ
Those people, I truly call f
and staying by my side.

For all
ahead. Add
those who
more difficu
inside a trea
For, if you d
necessary to
I've seen
didn't percei
simply keep
steps in their
that cycle by
My mess
freedom over
each step, the
of the steps b
us into who
I got into the
Serenity book.
the darkness a
able triumph o
had the slightes
deliverance.

If you are r
an addict, I hop
on in the mind
way we deal with
walks of life. For
It can depend o
the addiction, an
her life. In some
circumstances, it
you would be to
out of the addicti
ever give up.

Chapter One: Get a Clue

The first step in recovery, according to *The Twelve Steps of Alcoholics Anonymous*, is "We admitted we were powerless over alcohol, that our lives had become unmanageable." It was the easiest step for me. There were three things that really sent me over the edge and helped me hit bottom. The first thing was domestic violence. This is an issue for many women who self-medicate. I lived through several years of it. It began when I first met the father of my children, and lasted throughout our relationship. I do believe the worst part of domestic violence is not the physical abuse, but the horrible mental torture that the perpetrator seems to thoroughly enjoy. My husband was much more mentally abusive than physically, which caused hostility in our relationship. I was never prone to violent outbursts before in my life, until I began a relationship with this man. In the end, I questioned my own sanity. He seemed to enjoy watching me fall apart emotionally more than being physically abusive. Then, he would tell me that I was crazy and nobody could stand me, not even my own family. That was one way he thought he could secure our relationship. This would further alienate me from my loved ones. He told me he was the only one who'd put up with me. He would be physically, sexually and emotionally abusive to me until I forgot who I was and had no self –worth. We tried marital counseling, but the counselor asked him to step out of the room so she could speak with me alone. She said that she could not counsel him;

1

because his *MMPI* results showed that he was "anti –social with borderline sociopathic tendencies."

I remember an incident that occurred just prior to me leaving him for good. A few days before I checked myself into detox at the hospital, we got into one of those insane arguments that come with living in the cycle of addiction and domestic violence. I told him I didn't want to be with him anymore. I had ended a brief courtship with a younger man to give him another chance. I told him I was going to leave him, and the other guy never treated me like this. "That's why I know there's something wrong with our relationship, and I'm leaving!" I shouted. He hit me and I saw stars. I recall getting up from the floor thinking I had finally had enough. I was enraged and wanted him to die. Picking myself up off the floor, I ran into our bedroom. There was nothing going on in my mind that was intelligent or reasonable. I jumped up on the bed and unscrewed the heavy bedpost from the footboard and held it in my hand like a bat. I began yelling and cursing at him. I had every intention of hurting him. It felt like something else had taken over my body. My mother had already reported us to social services. That day I called them and let them know where to find us.

That's my last memory of our time together. Within a few days I was sitting in the hospital talking with a psychologist about this and telling her to help me. Within a couple of hours I was talking with a social worker. I pleaded with her, "If you will help us start over, I will do whatever it takes to better myself and make a peaceful life for my children," I pleaded. The caseworker made arrangements for me to transfer from detox to a shelter for battered women. The staff at the shelter was wonderful. I told them I wanted to find a treatment center like I'd seen on T.V. I thought I'd have to leave my children with family, but that was not the case. They soon found a place for me and my children to go where we could all receive therapy for trauma and my addiction.

After acquiring an attorney, I went before a judge to work out the legal custody issues, just to be sure that this wouldn't mean I'd have to give up the primary custody of my children. The custody papers were temporarily changed to ensure the father would have visitation with the children, as well. After six weeks in the shelter, I was relocated to the center. I have no regrets, and I never look back on my past with that man. However, I never let myself forget for fear that history will repeat itself.

The next thing that sent me downward was the guilt over the kind of parent I had become. You see, I was twenty-eight years old when I had my

This book is dedicated to Mary Ellen, for without her help, I wouldn't be here today.

I believe there are truly angels among us who work tirelessly to make lasting contributions to society and throw out lifelines to lost souls just trying to find their way.

I'm keeping my promise to you.

FOREWORD

Matthew 17:20 ..."for truly I say unto you, if you have faith the size of a mustard seed,
You will say to this mountain, 'Transfer from here to there, and it will transfer, and
Nothing will be impossible for you."

    This book is for all those struggling with addiction. It is not an autobiography, but a memoir of my journey through the twelve-step program. In each chapter, I will attempt to break down each step as it related to my life at the time. I hope I can provide insight into the process for both the addict and anyone trying to understand addiction and the recovery process. All information I am sharing is my opinion and is related to my personal journey. This is simply my story of how I came to perceive the steps, and how I worked them all. I hope that my story can be an inspiration and help to others.

    I would like to acknowledge my family and friends for all their support as I worked through all my struggles. I would like to send my grateful appreciation to those who didn't have to be there through my process, but chose to embrace me, educate me, or otherwise support me in my quest. Those people, I truly call friends. Thanks for standing in the gap for me and staying by my side.

For all the miles behind me, I realize there are still many more miles ahead. Addiction is simply kept at bay during the time of treatment. For those who have been to treatment centers, I believe the battle is so much more difficult when you leave treatment. There is an umbrella of protection inside a treatment facility. However, you must not take the situation lightly. For, if you do not work the steps, you most likely will not acquire the tools necessary to survive the process.

I've seen many terrible things happen in situations where the addict didn't perceive the serious nature of the problem. I've seen acquaintances simply keep using or drinking, which is a direct result of not working the steps in their lives. Hopefully, my story can help someone out there break that cycle by simplifying the steps to layman's terms.

My message is that it is through soul transformation that we find freedom over addiction. We simply use the Twelve Steps as a resource. For each step, there are scripture references that relate to the step. The working of the steps breaks down who we were (dysfunctional) and reconstructs us into who we become (functional). When I began working the steps, I got into the Bible, as well. I used many AA resources, including the *Serenity* book. All these resources together helped me find my way out of the darkness and into the light. Just as Matthew 17:20 promises, I was able triumph over my addiction, even though I had no faith in myself. I had the slightest faith in God, and that's all He needed me to have to find deliverance.

If you are reading this book because you are a friend or loved one of an addict, I hope my memoir will help you to understand what is going on in the mind of the addict. You see, we are all very much alike in the way we deal with life, yet we can be so different, as we come from different walks of life. For some, the process is just easier than it may be for others. It can depend on what the addiction was, how long the person was in the addiction, and how much the person really wants to transform his or her life. In some cases, there is great shame in being an addict. In other circumstances, it's the only life the addict has ever known. My advice to you would be to do whatever it takes to help that friend or loved one step out of the addiction. Each process is different. So, hang in there. Don't ever give up.

first child, and I promised God I would be a very good mother if He ever blessed me with children. I proceeded to have two of the most beautiful baby girls I had ever seen. I can remember leaving the hospital with my first child. As I was rolled down each hallway (in a wheelchair), I was feeling the mounting pressure inside of me that someone was going to take my baby at any moment. I thought, "How can they let me leave with this precious angel in my arms? Are they really going to let me keep her? Don't they know I don't deserve this wonderful child?"

I didn't drink or smoke when I was pregnant, but when I had them (fourteen months apart) I began to drink heavily. I also took anxiety medication for post –partum depression, which made it very difficult for me to function to my full capacity as a mother. I kept them clean and fed, but I was becoming more and more unattached as time went along, because the emotional toll was overwhelming. I never had any help from my husband or family at all. No one came to help me, and my husband just wanted me to make them stop crying.

So, I drank and popped those pills, becoming their servant instead of a mother. I resented the fact that I couldn't enjoy what I could never get a break from. It felt like an overly demanding job. I eventually became numb inside. I worried that I didn't love them enough. My husband never once changed a diaper, never rocked them to sleep, never read them a story. He used them as another form of torturing me. The more I would cry over the responsibility, the more he would laugh at me. He would tell me I was a bad mother.

I was also taking care of his two sons from his previous marriage. The only help I got came from them. They loved to help, but they were only nine and ten at the time, and I didn't want them to feel resentful, so I tried not to ask them for too much. They had endured so much, already. Their father took them away from their mother when they were three and four. She just didn't have the money to fight him in court, so he took them for leverage. Even during our relationship, he tormented her through limiting visitation with her children, moving so far way that it cost her so much money to see them. He also recorded all the phone conversations she had with them, listening to each recording every night when he came home from work. He loved all the drama. I felt like a terrible stepmother, because it was my responsibility to make sure the recorder was always recording. Not to mention, he didn't handle the discipline they needed. He said he wanted me to do it. Now, I believe it was just so they would resent me, thus causing *more* drama.

Finally, the third thing that sent me into treatment was the way my family chose to handle the situation. My sisters had stopped having anything to do with me by that point. My mother and father never disowned me for all the poor choices I had made in my life. They always tried to make some kind of contact with me off and on, just to know that I was alive and safe. Just before I decided to go to treatment, though, my mom told me I was cut off from the family until I could agree to go to treatment. She finally proclaimed that she and my dad had reached the end of their rope with me. MY INTERVENTION! I thank God for that day. I don't believe anyone wants to go into treatment and change everything they know as their life, but it's just the fear of the unknown that we, as addicts, must overcome. Our addiction is what we know, and detox is another kind of hell.

Intervention doesn't work for everyone, and neither does treatment. Still, the willingness to just accept the chaos of one's life and acknowledge the need to change is a good start. I remember calling my mom on the way to detox and telling her I was done. It was a liberating feeling to just acknowledge that I needed to change my life. No matter what treatment center I had to go to or what provisions would have to be made for the temporary care of my children, it would have been worth it. I think I would have succeeded in any treatment environment I may have been placed in, because I was already done in my mind. My husband and I were divorced for a couple of years, but had been back together for a few months, at that time. He dropped me off at the hospital, totally unaware of the fact that I had no intention of ever coming back.

There must be an acceptance of the fact that life is unmanageable, a desire to be different than the way we are, and a willingness to take action to complete step one. It is very simple. I remember the day that I arrived at the treatment center. I didn't know what to expect. What would the place look like? Where would my children and I sleep? Would the place be more violent than the environment I left? Would it be like a correctional facility? There were so many thoughts spinning around in my mind in route from one city to the next. A staff member from the shelter was kind enough to drive us that day, and she returned the truck after helping me unpack all my things into my new home. The shelter even paid for the cost of the move. I will forever remember that.

My children were sitting on the floor of the cab in the moving truck so excited to be going to the new life I had promised them. They kept looking up at me, smiling. I thought about all the instability they had endured in their short lives. I reflected on my own childhood, knowing that it wasn't perfect, but it was reasonably stable. How could I have been so selfish? Why would any mother put her kids through so much? When do we step up and say, "They depend on me for their very survival. It is my responsibility to be the grown –up and take care of them. I may not be perfect, but I'm all they were dealt in life. God expects me to do this. He blessed me with them." I felt blessed to have them at that moment, but I was totally aware of the fact that they were not so blessed to have me. The sad thing was, they loved me unconditionally. They didn't know I was a bad mother. I made a decision that moment that I would not leave this place no matter what happened, until it was time for me to go. I completed step one. I took action to set in motion certain changes in my life that were necessary to bring about the total change of me.

The first night after my arrival, I sat on my back porch (it was a nice deck) and looked up at the stars. There was a peaceful feeling in the air. Everything was quiet. All my neighbors had finished coming by to welcome me to the "neighborhood." There was no one tormenting me. I noticed that the neighborhood was fenced in, but I didn't feel trapped at all. I felt free. I cannot explain the freedom that a woman feels when she escapes her world of domestic violence. I have seen documentaries of women who served time for killing their husbands. I thank God for preserving my sanity so that was not the case for me. The stuff I left behind was meaningless to me. The people, places, and things I sacrificed for my recovery could never give me this feeling that I felt that night. It was the best decision I had ever made in my life to accept this gift of recovery.

I never saw those fences around the facility as anything but comforting. Some of the girls who had been in treatment for a while would make jokes about being "behind the gates" like they were missing something "out there." I saw the fences as a way to keep him out. I knew that I was finally in the one place where he couldn't hurt me, anymore.

I still woke up at night from nightmares, though. I had recurring dreams that I woke up and he was standing there looking at me. The first time I dreamed that, I was terrified. I went out on my front porch and pulled myself together. The security guard beat on my door at midnight to check my unit out (since I was new), and I thought it was him! I wouldn't go to the door until I was sure it really was the security guard. That is why I never saw those fences as cages or the facility as somewhere I didn't want to be.

5

I do recall that some of the other clients I had met that day seemed to have no sense of gratefulness to all the people who helped them. We all had some furniture that was donated by churches, social service agencies, and shelters. I was disturbed by the attitudes some of the girls had. I sat in my bed that night and prayed that God would never let me forget all the many resources He had blessed me with. I think that because I made all these calls myself, I was slightly more aware of all the effort it takes to start over. My advice to women in shelters in the same situation I was in is to do your own 'leg –work.' Agencies like women's shelters are there to provide the service of safety. Don't become comfortable and dependent on the staff and facility for your future well –being. Get a phone book, and do what you need to do to change your circumstances. God created us to be strong and self –sufficient. Get up and do something about it!

I am not proud of the life I lived in my addiction. When I entered treatment, I wanted to be in denial. I regretted all my mistakes and just wanted to move forward and forget the past. Step One is about working through your denial and totally accepting your life as it is, good and bad. We can't just stop living in addiction and "close the door" on our pasts. If we do that, we have no point to grow from. We also have nothing to remind us why we stay sober. I have had friends and relatives who have lost weight and kept a picture on the refrigerator of the way they looked before the weight loss. Every one of them would say, "I have to remind myself how overweight I was so that I don't forget to eat right." So, my advice to others at this crucial step is to take a mental picture of yourself, now. This is what you will keep reflecting on throughout your process.

Chapter 2: Where's Your Faith?

As a preacher's kid, I knew all about the Bible. I knew all about church. When I entered treatment, I didn't need anyone to tell me about God. On the other hand, I felt abandoned by God. You see, I didn't have this stone hard heart that couldn't be saved. I just didn't know He would save me. I hadn't truly come to conceive of God's grace. Step two, according to The Twelve Steps of Alcoholics Anonymous, states "Came to believe that a power greater than ourselves could restore us to sanity." I'm not going to mislead you on that one. I was actually in treatment for three-and-a-half months before I was able to master step two. In treatment, each step is worked one step at a time. There are group activities that help you see where you are at in the process. So, we remained on step one for some time before moving to step two. It was during a group therapy session that another consumer said to me, "If God was ready to throw you away, then He wouldn't have brought you here. Don't you see? He had grace to carry you until you could see what was going on." That was the turning point for me. I was so excited that God still standing there after all those years. I found a friend, eventually, when I was able to leave on day passes to work who invited me to church. She came and picked me up every Sunday, faithfully, for the remainder of the time I was in the facility. She and her husband even came to help me move when I finished the program. God was placing his servants in my path to throw out the lifeline and save my soul. I was grabbing that lifeline, too. I was saved in their church about nine months before I finished my treatment. That's not to say that I became this perfect person all at once. I still continued to make mistakes, but through it all I never gave in to my addiction. I managed to be very successful in that respect. It was my defects of character that I continued to wrestle with. My God is still working on me to this day, and I'm still listening. Working this step will require you to do some letting go. You got your life in this mess, so how do you think you can fix it. When I tell my children to clean their playroom after they've made a really big mess, they look at me bewildered and say," Can you help us, Mommy? The mess got too big!" We do the same thing with our lives. Do you think I don't help my children clean up the mess? I do most of the work! So, for those of you who do not believe in God, I realize there is some controversy to this matter. Hence, this is my memoir of my experiences. I can only share with you my experiences, strength and hope. Consequently, I must say that my Higher Power is God. For the sake of argument, I can say nothing more. You must work step two before you can move on to step three, because it's going to take a Higher Power to help you do that! Good luck to you!

Chapter Three: Giving up the Wheel

"We perceive that only through utter defeat are we able to take our first steps toward liberation and strength…"
Twelve Steps and Twelve Traditions, p. 21

Step three is a hard step for those who have found life to be full of tragedy or great difficulties. Trusting others is difficult for those who have been molested as a child, abused in their lifetimes, or otherwise have suffered incidents that may have caused them to have trust issues. I can't say that I suffered horrible things in my childhood. I wasn't tortured or abused. My parents were young and energetic. They were together since high school, married and had three children. Eventually, my dad went into the ministry. He was a very devoted husband and father. Of course, he still is. My mother is a very strong woman. She is grounded in her life and her faith in God. She never was a drinker, smoker, or drug addict. I had a respectable family that I didn't have to be ashamed of when I was a child.

The only traumatic thing that happened in my life -besides domestic violence- was the night that I was kidnapped by a serial rapist. On New Year's Eve of 1995, I found myself in that situation. I don't want to recall every detail of the incident, but I did manage to get away from this man before he raped me. God was with me that night. He gave me strength and wit to escape the situation, and He helped me find my way out of the woods once I managed to get free from the situation. It was a very long ordeal, and is hard to talk about, even now. I only mention the incident to share with you the grace of God, because He was there to see me through.

He saw me through that situation and many more that I helped create, either through being in the wrong place at the wrong time, or just making bad decisions overall.

Turning my will over to God was hard for me, because I didn't take responsibility for my mistakes. How can you surrender something you don't realize you own? When I was new in treatment, I found myself talking a lot about things I knew nothing about. I blamed people in my past for the way I turned out in my life. I blamed my ex-husband for my addiction. One day in group, another consumer pointed out to me that I was an addict and my ex-husband couldn't be made to bear the responsibility of my addiction. She suggested that I would've still been an addict had I been with a different man. Maybe if I'd been in a relationship with a heroin addict, I may have even become addicted to heroin. The underlying factors bore no relevance to the fact that I was an addict, so I had to accept that before I could begin to surrender this to God.

Taking responsibility for your choices must precede your surrender. Then, you must be willing to believe that you will continue to make the same mistakes over and over again unless you give up and give God control of your actions. If you follow the will of God, He will guide you in your course in life. This takes a conscious connection with Him. I began to think of consequences before I would make decisions to do things. God will prick your heart if you are about to make a bad decision. You must listen to your conviction or you'll take the wrong route.

We have a tendency to just "go with the flow" and do whatever our impulses trigger us to do if we don't surrender our will to God. There is a saying in recovery, "If you always do what you've always done, you'll always get what you always got." Mistakes don't have to keep reoccurring in our lives. We just have to make better choices along the way.

This principle can be applied to the lives of people with any sort of recurring problem.

When I surrendered my will to God, things began to change in my life. I felt freedom in my surrender. I no longer had to wake up with guilt about my lifestyle. I had something to be excited about. I felt like staying in my home with children watching movies and making treats. I realized that I liked being content, and I didn't feel the need to seek satisfaction in other things such as karaoke, shooting pool, and trying new alcoholic beverages.

I came into treatment with two bibles. They were both bartenders' bibles. I left treatment with one Bible. It was the Holy Bible. I don't feel ashamed to be a Christian, but I did feel ashamed of who I was before I surrendered my will to God. I came in a shell of a person, but after 18 months of treatment, I was sure of myself. I believed I would be okay. I knew I could count on God, and He would never fail me. I wasn't afraid I would relapse, because I knew who was on my side.

"*True ambition is not what we thought it was. True ambition is the deep desire to live usefully and walk humbly under the grace of God.*" (Twelve Steps and Twelve Traditions) pp124-125. I have trouble sympathizing with those "in recovery" that get the wrong message from the invitation to "*keep coming back.*" I know some people who believe that means to keep picking up "white chips" (tokens in AA given to newcomers and those who've slipped and have to start over). These people don't understand the fact that working your recovery means just that: WORKING your recovery. Now, I'm not trying to discourage anyone or be judgmental. However, "*there are such unfortunates*" means that not everyone is going to apply these twelve principles to their lives. Attitudes of indifference or intolerance towards these principles are what I'm making reference to. Do you really want sobriety or not?

What my frustration is with these people is that they are wasting the time of everyone involved in their recoveries. I want to send out a message to those people who don't take recovery seriously. For those who have attended meetings for several years and can't seem to get past the "white chip," Have you surrendered, yet? Remember what the third edition of Alcoholics anonymous reads on page 542, "*...there are only two sins; the first is to interfere with the growth of another human being, and the second is to interfere with one's own growth.*" Now, in pointing this out, I'm not trying to discourage anyone who may be having problems staying on the wagon. My point is that you have to get on and stay on at some point in the game. Get on the wagon and hold on. Put some effort into your attempt to stay sober.

According to the book *A.A. Comes of Age*, we are rescued by surrendering. There is a passage on page 311 that reads, "*...Inwardly the alcoholic brooks no control from man or God. He, the alcoholic, is and must be the master of his destiny. He will fight to the end to preserve that position.*" There really is no control in addiction. You may always think that you'll handle yourself differently *this time* like you can choose to be in charge of your capacities once you surrender to your addiction, but you can't control yourself without clarity of mind. You will always act the same way, every time you give your addiction control until it eventually kills you.

Today, I completely rely on God for my sobriety. I still find myself in situations of extreme temptation. Just the other day, I found myself in a store paying for gas after dark. My kids and I had been shopping and I was frustrated and tired. While waiting in line, my kids started begging for a drink from an ice packed display in front of us. The sign read "**Three for \$1.00**" It looked like a good deal, so I was about to grab them both a drink, when I realized it was beer in the display. My heart leaped! Beer that cheap? I had to surrender control to God immediately. My favorite song is *"Jesus take the Wheel"* by Country artist Carrie Underwood. I can't count the times I've had to pray that very prayer just to survive a moment. My children had no control of whether or not I'd make a bad choice, but God did. Surrender in each situation is vital to survival of addiction.

When I was at the battered women's shelter, I received donations from a church, Children and Family Services, the shelter, and Habitat for Humanity to get started on my own. I knew I had lots of good people praying for me that I would do well, and I didn't want to let those people down. However, when I gave myself to God, He became my everything and it was God I didn't want to let down. God was the only one left standing when everyone else had forsaken me. When others turned from me, He was there. He was my friend when I had no friends, my family when I had no family and my companion when I was all alone against the world. I'm so glad I surrendered myself to Him. I would never have known the serenity there is in allowing God full control if I had not surrendered to Him that day in church.

If you are having trouble with step three, let me assure you it is the easiest part of the process. Sure, you may have been left broken by someone or everyone in your life so far, but trusting your Higher Power will empower you in your life. There is no greater freedom than surrendering to God. He's a friend that will stick closer than a brother. Consider the passage from page 47 in *Alcoholics Anonymous,* 'We need to ask ourselves but one short question. "Do I now believe, or am I even willing to believe, that there is power greater than myself?" As soon as a man can say that he does believe, or is willing to believe, we emphatically assure him that he is on his way.'

Chapter Four: Digging Deep

"All these failings generate fear, a soul sickness in its own right."
Twelve Steps and Twelve Traditions p. 49

The hardest thing to do in anyone's recovery is to see who you really are inside. It's like looking in the mirror at a disfigured face. You can't learn to love yourself enough to change your character defects unless you are willing to acknowledge the image of yourself that everyone else can easily see. To make a "searching and fearless moral inventory" of yourself, as the fourth step instructs, you may need a sponsor. It is important to have a sponsor as soon as possible in your recovery, but it is particularly important that you have one before you attempt step four. I went through a few during this time.

I remember this time in my recovery process being awfully difficult for me. It seemed like there was a lot of work involved, and I was confused. How do you begin to do a moral inventory? What are you supposed to be looking for? Are you supposed to recall every single thing you ever did wrong in your life? It is helpful to use resources during this process. I was in a treatment facility at this time, so my resources were provided by the facility. I remember doing worksheets throughout this procedure, and I'm glad I was in a safe environment the whole time. It was after I began step four that I struggled the most with my emotional solidity, so I was placed on a "suicide contract." The staff just had to take precautions, because I had a lot of baggage from my experiences of personal trauma.

What I didn't realize, at first, was the fact that the step wasn't about listing acts of wrongdoing as much as it was about discovering the underlying character defects causing me to make poor choices and commit wrong acts. Once I began to accept that I was a dysfunctional individual, I could begin to cultivate changes in my actions. One phrase that was popular in the facility at that time was "act as if..." I began to "act as if" I was willing, until I truly became willing. I had to "act as if" I liked sitting at home alone with my children, until I realized one day that I did enjoy doing that. I also had to "act as if" I had self –esteem, until I developed a positive self –image.

The purpose of doing a "searching and fearless moral inventory is to get to the core of what makes us dysfunctional in our lives. Why must we consume drugs or alcohol to the extent of self –destruction just to endure the agony of Life? I believe that we must apply certain changes in our behavior to overcome the self –deception and self –pity that unravels us over time. We don't just wake up one morning an alcoholic. The progression from functional to dysfunctional occurs over a period of years. Therefore, it may actually take a considerable amount of time to regain the sturdiness in our lives that help us maintain our sobriety.

During this time of self –insight, it is important to remember that you are not alone. *"Finally, we begin to see that all people , including ourselves, are to some extent emotionally ill as well as frequently wrong, and then we approach true tolerance and see what real love for our fellows actually means."* (Twelve Steps and Twelve Traditions) p. 92. We begin to look around at others, at some point, and we can feel empathy for others in recovery.

I remember calling my mom and telling her that I finally realized that I had nothing to feel sorry for myself about, when there were so many other people in treatment with me who had suffered so much more tragedy in their lives than I had. Self –deception and self –pity are common defects of character for those of us in recovery.

I cannot finish this chapter without touching on some of my most significant character defects. The first is **pride.** With God's help, I had to transform arrogance, conceit, and self-importance to self –respect, dignity, and self –esteem. There was a dysfunction in my concept of pride. Working out this step helped me change my concept of pride, therefore, making the changes crucial to overcoming this character defect. I came into treatment with no sense of self –worth, unable to smile and laugh. I felt pitiful, yet when it came to accepting responsibility for my behavior, I just couldn't do that. My arrogance, conceit, and self–importance caused me to blame others for my addiction.

Another defect of character that I discovered within myself was **inferiority**. Feelings of inferiority caused me to become the way I was, to begin with. I sought approval from the wrong crowd. I never felt *cool* like others. I always felt beneath everyone else around me, even though I "hung out" with people who possessed no moral character. According to ***The Language of the Heart***, "*This very real feeling of inferiority is magnified by his childish sensitivity and it is this state of affairs which generates in him that insatiable, abnormal craving for self–approval and success in the eyes of the world.*" (p. 102) I had a hole in me that could never be filled. There is an emptiness and loneliness in a person who carries this complex of inferiority, a feeling of being invisible and invalidated as a person. Unless this changes, the person will have no real feeling of happiness in life.

The very worst defect of character that I posses is **anger**. No matter how hard I try, that one is the hardest to overcome. I have an awful temper! I know that I will spend every day of the rest of my life trying to overcome this character defect. I was diagnosed with post–traumatic stress disorder several years ago. I continue to suffer the aftermath of having been a victim of kidnapping in 1995. I had to stab the guy to get away from him, but I know in my heart that it was necessary for my survival to do this. He intended to kill me that night, and I would not have been the first person he had killed, as I was later informed.

That experience, combined with surviving domestic violence, caused instability in my nervous system. Now, the very sound of a slamming door causes me to jump out of my skin. If the kids get too noisy, my husband turns the television all the way up. All the noise triggers my PTSD. I don't think anyone realizes how I really feel inside when this occurs. I begin to feel like I'm going to go over the edge. The room starts spinning and all the sound combines together like a loud, intolerable wind. My frustration turns to rage if I can't make it stop soon. Since I did step four, I've began to use breathing and visualization techniques to intercede and prevent myself from "losing it."

There are so many more defects of character that I have had to work on since I began this journey to recovery. Sometimes, it is very simple to correct a flaw by simply changing an undesirable behavior such as gossip. Other times, the defect is so severe that it can only be corrected by God. I believe there are some things I've actually had to be delivered from. Only a cleansing of my sole could change my self –centered attitude, and the feeling of emptiness that caused me to suffer an inferiority complex could only be overcome by the paradox of the salvation experience.

This step will never be done and over with. Yet, in taking on our personal demons, we become empowered to overcome them. To face ourselves in the mirror and make a decision to change the image before us is what I believe step four is all about. I still find myself fighting the same temptations every day that I've always fought. Sometimes, I still want to get in someone's face about my children, go off the handle about being overcharged for something, or defend myself in a "ghetto –fabulous" fashion. I don't always make the right choices, but I can reflect on my original self –inventory and add to it as I discover more things about myself that I need to change.

An important thing to note in this chapter is the fact that when we "dry out," we still carry around "addictive behaviors." Before these behaviors can begin to change, we must experience a change of our inner selves. *"We recovered alcoholics are not so much brothers in virtue as we are brothers in our defects, and in our common strivings to overcome them"* (As Bill Sees It) p.167.

Without doing the fourth step in the recovery process, there is not much hope for overall change, in my opinion. I think this is why so many people continue to fail in recovery. An "attitude of indifference or intolerance" can thwart recovery from taking place. When you apply step one to your life, you simply admit that your life has become unmanageable. By continuing the process through steps two and three, you accept that God must be in control of your life, because you make a mess of it on your own. Nevertheless, step four is when the healing begins. All your fears, resentments, and shortcomings come out on the table. When you do this, God takes control. I am an example of God turning "trash" to "treasure." He has been taking all my defects of character from me and replacing them with inner resources.

Chapter Five: The truth will set you free.

"…When it comes to ego deflation, few steps are harder to take than Five.
But scarcely any step is more necessary to longtime sobriety and peace of mind than this one."

Twelve Steps and Twelve Traditions p.55

Step five happened for me. Once I worked step four, I wanted to tell my wrongdoings to someone. I had been holding things inside of myself that were keeping me from being able to love me. Addiction is a burden. There is shame in the fact, alone, that I am an addict. Add to that shame the things I did when I was drunk or high, and you can imagine the guilt I had to live with. I don't care what any addict claims, people who are in active addiction do not take care of the needs of their children. The biggest area of guilt for me was the kind of mother I had become in the end. Certainly, I can recall good things I did for my children. Yet, when one must balance the good with the bad, let's be real. I was no "Mommy of the Year." There must be a total honesty when you share your experiences with others. "The *exact nature* of our wrongs" meant to me that I was not going to be able to "sugar –coat" what kind of mother, wife, sister, daughter, granddaughter, or friend I had been in my addiction.

I think it is very important to every addict in the process of recovery to be very wise about how they work step five. I broke up the list from step four and made decisions about whom I would share this information with. After all, do you really want to expose in a group setting how you "found ways and means to use," if those ways were to include criminal activity? You have to be careful about how and to whom you expose certain information.

If you committed a crime, there may be an obligation on someone else's part to turn you in. I'm not saying that I had robbed anyone or violated the law in my addiction. I am simply saying that there are ways to work this step without becoming vulnerable in a meeting or group setting. I chose to seek professional counseling during this time just to talk about things that I could not fully disclose in group. For example, I made the mistake of sharing the story of my kidnapping in group, only to be scoffed at by the others who didn't believe my story. You must keep in mind that the others in a group setting are most likely not professional psychologists, and they can be brutal in their judgment of you. I later had to discuss the events of my kidnapping with a professional who was able to help me heal from the emotional burden I had been carrying around for years. Separate the information and don't just be so forthcoming in the wrong environment. It can cause a setback in your recovery, if not a relapse.

I believe that step five is about saying out loud all those things you know about yourself that keep you bound in your addiction. Remember, though, step five is about *your* defects of character. Don't make the mistake of sharing the exact nature of someone else's wrongs. I mean, you want to get to the core of your own problem, not someone else's. It is tempting to make excuses for your behaviors and character defects, but you can't heal if you don't work steps four and five right. I believe that these two steps are fundamental in the 12 step process. With that being said, be very honest with yourself and others about your character. You can't change negative elements of your moral fiber unless you are completely honest.

It's hard to paint a real picture of how difficult these steps were for me to work through. I can say to every addict out there reading this book that I know what you are going through. For me, only God could heal the pain I was suffering. Only He could salvage the mess I had made of my life. My healing, my power, my deliverance, and my resilience to overcome this addiction came from God. Every time I shared in a meeting, God gave me more buoyancy to persevere. Once a weak, pitiful shell of a human being, I was slowly transformed through the empowerment of the Holy Spirit.

I felt like the 'woman at the well' in the Bible. After she met Jesus at the well, she ran through the town telling everyone about the man who gave her living water. I found no bounty in drugs or alcohol, but Christ filled me with a sense of quintessence that I was trying to find in substances. "Wash me, and I will be whiter than snow" (Psalm 51:7). I was once lost in a dark place, but I was free. The freedom was unexplainable. I'm sure I can imagine the woman at the well that day that she met Jesus. I can picture her running back through the town feeling several pounds lighter, like her feet were coming up off the ground. She probably couldn't even help it. She had to run. I imagine she looked up at the sky, and it looked so blue and beautiful. The leaves on the trees were probably a different shade of green than she had seen before. There was a great feeling of victory in her soul as she felt the fresh air breeze through her hair – air that smelled different and felt cleaner. Can you imagine how it would feel to meet Jesus face to face? Yes, my life may have been dark and meaningless before, but I could share with others the exact nature of my wrongs, because I had been set free.

I can imagine the woman at the well saying, "I had been married and divorced several times and was even now living with a man who was not my husband, but Jesus gave me something that none of those guys could ever give me. I'm free! I'm free!" When she found freedom from her sins, she had a testimony to share. As a result, she introduced others to this Savior. They knew that a change had truly taken place in her, because they saw the transformation in this woman. I'm sure that many others in that small town came to know Christ as a result of her personal experience at the well that day.

In step one I had to admit that my addiction was in control of me. I had no power over my addiction. I no longer took care of the responsibilities of my life, including my obligations to my children to keep them fed, safe, clean, and warm. As hard as it was to accept that this was my life, I had to admit it. Then, in step two, I came to believe that a power greater than myself could restore me to sanity. This was a process that took several months. I didn't just accept that right away. God had to begin to reveal Himself to me in many different ways. After this revelation that God was waiting for me to open the door and accept Him into my heart, I naturally worked step three. Having done that step, I had to do step four. I couldn't be Christian if I held on to all those defects of character. So, with Gods help, I kept writing down my personality defects as He showed them to me. This was process that took a considerable amount of time. I had to display these defects for God to show me that they were there. My behaviors couldn't change until the core of me began to change. Finally, I could work step five. To talk about things at meetings like how I treated someone that day or something I did that I knew I shouldn't have done was helping me to be able to change those things. After telling on myself at a meeting, I thought about it the next time I was in the situation. Suddenly, I began noticing that my thinking process was changing. This is what happens when you work through steps 1 through 5. You just begin to notice these changes in yourself.

When you work step five, there are some things you have to keep between yourself and God. If I included everything about my life in this book with total transparency, I would never finish the book. I also wouldn't want to expose "all" to everyone in the world.

I believe Jesus disappeared to the wilderness to be tempted by Satan so that it would stay between Himself and Satan. If His disciples had been there, they would have seen Jesus in a more vulnerable, powerless kind of way. Not to mention the distraction they would have caused with all their advice, questions, and criticism. Jesus would've had twice the pressure on Him to obey the will of God with all that added confusion. There are some things I believe God doesn't expect us to share with others for that very reason. People have good intentions most of the time, but some people will use the very thing you expose about yourself to cause you harm or work against you. If Jesus could've had faith in His disciples like He had in God the Father, they would've been by His side during His temptation in the wilderness.

I can't stress enough the importance of using discretion and wisdom in working this step. Confidentiality is important in recovery, especially when working steps four and five. Relapse prevention is one reason for this. The things I can't trust others with, I can give to God. Isaiah 41: 10 reads, "So do not fear, for I am with you; do not be dismayed, for I am your God. I will strengthen you and help you; I will hold you up with my righteous right hand." Sometimes, we just have to realize that God can do what no psychiatrist or well –meaning person in our life can do for us. Our faith will set us free.

The thing to strive for in working step five is recognizing yourself for all that you are and being forthcoming with God, yourself, and another person. This way, you begin to experience the consciousness to make changes in yourself. You should already have the clarity by this point, if you have stayed sober throughout this period. Share what you can with others so that they can be helped through your experiences, strength and hope. Recognize when to be honest with yourself and with God. Listen to others who have more experience and wisdom. Make it to meetings and to church. It takes dedication to see liberation from such a thing as bad as addiction. Everything in you wants to fall back on instant gratification that you found in your addiction. To make it past the point of continually revisiting familiar things, you must thoroughly work step five.

You must be careful while still early in your recovery not to romance your addiction. I think this is a good place to mention that there is a difference in sharing experiences and *admitting* things about you in hope to *change* personal defects and *romancing* addiction. There was nothing funny or exciting to me about my addiction, yet there was a personal deception for me in the correct way to disclose this information. When I talked about the things I did in my addiction, others would laugh and be triggered to share their own stories in an inappropriate way. We were instructed by the staff at the treatment center to be careful with this, because of the deception of addiction. You may unwittingly begin to miss getting drunk or high by sharing "funny" stories, forgetting the final details in those situations. Yes, I had fun at a party one afternoon with my girlfriends. We got crazy singing karaoke and ended up in the pool having a splashing good time. It was hilarious when we were able to call the liquor store and have more alcohol delivered to us for $100 tip. However, I nearly drowned when I passed out in the pool and my face was hanging off the side of my float in the water. Everyone else was too drunk to notice. If a friend's husband hadn't come by to "check on the girls," I wouldn't have been pulled from the water in time before I drowned. Or, what about the time I drove through town with my lights off, because I was too drunk to realize that they weren't on? That wouldn't have been so funny if I had caused a wreck or ran over a pedestrian.

There is no humor in the devastation of addiction. I remember a time when I was in treatment that we went on a shopping trip to Wal Mart. I grabbed my bags on the way out the door, leaving my shopping cart behind. Once I got in the parking lot, I realized my bags were too heavy. Grabbing the first cart I could find, I was relieved to rid myself of the weight of the bags in my arms. Then, I noticed that there was an empty box in the front of the cart. It had an "Icehouse" label on the cover and had contained a twelve –pack of beer bottles. Instead of removing this empty box, I left it there and proceeded back to the vehicle. I got the whole group of consumers in trouble, and we nearly lost the privilege of enjoying future outings like this. I didn't consider what was wrong about what I had done, at that time. I wouldn't do the same thing today. There were people who were new to the center that may have been triggered by that very stupid thing I did. I thought it was funny, but later struggled with my old demons, seeking counseling for the effects that episode had on my own recovery.

Even in our recovery, we continue to make mistakes that could potentially devastate our recuperation. It is important to realize that admitting the exact nature of our wrongs is an ongoing process. We never complete this step, because we never stop doing wrong things. Keep coming back to this one as you continue in your recovery.

Chapter Six: Clean Slate

"Cleanse me from my sin!" (Psalm 51:2)

There are many sins we want to hold onto in our recovery. We justify those things that we don't want to let go of. As stated by the **Twelve Steps and Twelve Traditions** (p.65), *"If we ask, God will certainly forgive our derelictions. But in no case does He render us white as snow and keep us that way without our cooperation."* In step six, we are submitting ourselves fully to the will of God, surrendering our sins over to Him. He will take the pain, the guilt, and the shame of our past from us, but we have to surrender the sinful behavior and be willing to change our ways to continue to move forward in our recovery.

When I got to the place in my recovery of wholly surrendering my sins to God, I was already out of the treatment facility. I didn't experience a total transformation all at once. However, I did believe going into treatment that I would come out 'cured' from addiction. I had to discover the hard way that it doesn't work like that. There were many things I said and did while I was still in the facility that I'm ashamed of. My behavior was sometimes immature and inappropriate. While working the job I had as a waitress, I still displayed some character flaws in my interaction with customers that I did eventually surrender to God. I would flirt with men, act rude if I felt wronged, and use inappropriate language at times, just to name a few things. I have mentioned my inappropriate behavior towards the staff at the facility, already. For every negative behavior I demonstrated, there was an underlying character flaw. I believe God will continue to make changes in me as I continue to cooperate with His will in my life.

Step Six of the Twelve Steps of Alcoholics Anonymous states, *"Were entirely ready to have God remove all these defects of character."* I wanted to be someone better than the person I knew myself to be. I prayed, "God take this from me. I don't want this anymore!" God did take it from me, beginning with the desire. My desire changed. I no longer desired to drink. I no longer felt the urge to swallow a handful of pills. Gone were the days of trying things at parties to fit in with people who were beneath my principled background. I didn't need to look for validation in all the wrong circumstances. I found my most valuable validation from God. It is an awesome feeling to know you are known and loved by a being greater than any man. To be set free from your transgressions by God will change your desires. You will begin to desire things like a home, a family, and meaningful relationships with others. As these changes take place in your spirit, your attitude will begin to change. I became a more humble person over time, no longer needing to be the one on top in every conflict I had with others.

Another change that took place in me was the way I dressed. I now think I should try to wear clothing that reflects a mom in her thirties, as opposed to a sexy partying type. The way you dress reflects the way you feel about yourself as a person. I gained more self–respect over time, therefore, I dress more respectably. I also have the means to dress myself, since I am no longer investing in my addiction. When I first went into treatment, everything I wore reflected the image of an alcoholic. My clothes were the last remnants of a certain lifestyle. I slowly began to change my wardrobe, because I would put on an outfit and think, "Man, I look too wild in this!" I believe God took the desire from me to party, so I no longer wanted to look the part. My lifestyle changed as my attitude toward life changed.

The hardest thing for me to surrender to God was my ego. The most self–destructive flaw within me was my own sense of pride and accomplishment when I would go for a while without drinking. I had periods of sobriety that I took full credit for in my past. I could manage to stay sober for a while, but not for good. I failed in all my attempts at sobriety, because I had not surrendered to God. Obadiah 1: 3- 4 reads, *"The pride of your heart has deceived you, you who live in the clefts of the rocks and make your home on the heights, you who say to yourself, 'Who can bring me to the ground?' Though you soar like the eagle and make your nest amongst the stars, from there I will bring you down."* God has ways of deflating egos. By the time I surrendered my ego to God, I was about to "bottom –out" in my recovery. I came close to relapse right before I finished the treatment program I was in. It took me some time to realize that my ego was the problem, but God was finally able to reveal that to me through allowing me to fall off my "high horse."

If I could say that there was a "cure –all" for addiction, or there was a secret that every addict should know, it would be the awesome power of God. God is my healer, my deliverer. His presence is always at the forefront of my life. He must be first, and I must be last. The only I way I know to stay sober is to die to yourself and live in Christ. I have seen others fail, lose the custody of their children, or end up in prison because of their addictions. I know that the missing thing in their situations was humility. I know that they were trying to stay sober through their own capacity. Some of these acquaintances didn't profess faith in a Higher Power, only in themselves. I was once one of the unfortunate souls drifting along this way, until I made this observation. I didn't want that to be me, so I surrendered.

Chapter Seven: Finding Virtue

"My creator, I am now willing that you should have all of me, good and bad."

Alcoholics Anonymous (p.76)

Shortcomings – inadequacies, failings, faults, deficiencies, limitations, weaknesses, the opposite of virtues. Wow! We *all* have faults. Everyone experiences limitations. To recognize our limitations, we must endure some opposition in our lives. That is when we find out what inadequacies we posses. One of my problem areas was, of course, decision making. I didn't always act as an advocate for my children. I lived with them in a home where there was domestic violence. I will always remember an incident when my ex –husband assaulted me in our vehicle one morning in front of my nine – month –old baby. He pulled my head down into his fist between the front seats of our minivan. He broke my glasses into my face. I got up and got away from him, got out of the van, and was unbuckling my baby from her car seat, when he suddenly began backing up with my baby dangling from the car seat by only a seatbelt strap. She has a nervous condition to this day from that incident. She was terrified and screaming. Of course, the sheriff's department in that county was pathetic. I believed that most of them were going home at night and beating their wives.

Needless to say, this man that I was married to at the time was never arrested for domestic violence, except on that occasion. He had a scratch on his back, so I was arrested along with him. Even though he hung up on the 911 call six times, he was never charged with a felony. I was kept in the infirmary on a mat on the floor, because I was eight months pregnant.

That incident alone should have ended my relationship with that man, but it didn't.

I left him for a while until he started harassing my family and straining my relationship with them. I found it easier to stay with him than to endure the agony of trying to escape him. Over time, I stayed in shelters for battered women, with his parents, even moved to Florida to stay with distant cousins, but there was no escape from my dark life.

Once in treatment, I discovered that I was co –dependent on him. Through counseling, I began to recover my sense of self –worth and self –sufficiency. I became empowered with the tools I began to acquire. I became educated about the cycle of domestic violence and the devastating effects it had on the children in those situations. Finally, I began to be the kind of advocate I needed to be for my children. They are vulnerable, because they do not have a voice in the situation. We, as mothers, must be the voice for our children. We must protect them. It is a mother's responsibility to provide a safe home for her children. Once I realized that, I began to make plans to change my home environment. I knew that returning to that life could not be an option for me after completing the program. With God's help, I corrected that area of deficiency in myself.

There was a time in my life when everything had to be about me. Now, I think of my children first. Before I do something, I think about the effect it will have on my children. I am aware of their needs. I bathe them, feed them, provide decent clothing for them to wear, and nurture them. When God changed me, my children had a new mother. I will not easily forget my sins as God did, so I have been guilty of "going overboard" making it up to them.

Now, having "humbly asked Him to remove our shortcomings," we will go through different developmental stages in our recovery.

While in treatment, I started out very cooperative with the program. I never wanted to go backwards in my recovery, so I resisted the temptation to relapse. I got through the hard times by communicating with the staff and reaching out when I thought I was having difficulties. It was during the end of my treatment that I began to have problems. I don't know to this day what was wrong with me, just that I became extremely agitated with the staff as a whole, even the daycare center staff on site. I can only speculate that I was becoming stagnant there and needed to move on into society, beginning my after –care plan. I began to feel "stuck" in a place where I had the tools I needed to be successful in my recovery, but was continuously held back by my behavior. My character defect was resentment. It manifested itself as hostility, aggression, and enmity toward others. God had to take that defect from me.

The good thing about giving up our shortcomings to God is the fact that for every defect of character God removes from our moral fiber, He replaces it with a quality. We simply trade our defects of character for eminence. *"You were taught, with regard to your former way of life, to put off your old self, which is being corrupted by its deceitful desires; to be made new in the attitude of your minds; and to put on the new self, created to be like God in true righteousness and holiness."* (Ephesians 4: 22-24). As it goes on to say further in these scriptures, we begin to lose those defects of character and evolve into better creatures as we draw closer to Christ in our spirits. This was the only way I could transform my character.

I believe there is no other way to defeat addiction than to be transformed in our souls. I have witnessed many hopeless cases continue to fail time and again, because of an unwillingness to part ways with the sin of addiction. I cannot say that I will just "try" to stay sober "just for today," only to decide to give in to my addiction tomorrow. Recovery is not for the weak at heart. It takes effort on our part to stay "on the wagon." After all, is my faith stronger in the God who delivered me or in the addiction that deceived me? We must surrender ourselves wholly to God, trading our shortcomings for virtues.

I had a long list of shortcomings. Today, I still struggle with defects of character. However, there is great hope in the fact that "God is my refuge and strength, an ever present help in the time of trouble."(Psalm 46:1) He has continued to strive with me and He continues to show me when I do wrong. It takes messing up, sometimes, to be corrected. When I say or do something that could potentially hinder my recovery, god is right there to deal with me, revealing my errors. Through divine revelation from God, I can continue to grow and change even my personality. After all, my personality is simply a reflection of my moral fiber. Once my character flaws began to depart, my intrinsic worth began to spring forth.

No matter how bad you believe you are, or how difficult it will be for you to change, nothing is impossible for God. Step seven is about surrendering your shortcomings to God. Its okay to be lazy and allow God to do the work in you. If you are like me, you'll be amazed and wonder how He did it. I just sit back in awe, knowing that I *must* give all the glory to God that I am changed today. I have to be honest: I don't remember *doing* anything! I simply surrendered myself to Him. It's amazing what God can do when we trust Him.

Chapter Eight: Becoming Willing

"Some of us, though, tripped over a very different snag. We clung to the claim that when drinking we never hurt anybody but ourselves."
Twelve Steps And Twelve Traditions, p. 79

Step eight of the Twelve Steps reads, "Made a list of all persons we had harmed, and became willing to make amends to them all." I began making my list, and three months later, I had completed the list. I realized that there was no way to reach some of the people I had harmed in my addiction, so I tried to seek forgiveness from the ones I still had some contact with. Then, I prayed that God would forgive me for the sins against the ones I could no longer reach out to. I found some consolation in doing for others. I began to help people around me, both inside and outside the treatment facility. Doing for others was so rewarding to me that I continued this behavior, and I still find solace in it to this day.

Humility is the goal of step eight. When you forgive another person, you rid yourself of the corrosiveness of resentment. When you receive forgiveness from another person, you are set free from the corrosiveness of guilt. Two feelings many addicts carry inside are resentment and guilt. Forgiveness mends the soul of the forgiven. There is hurt in harming others that we in addiction feel, as well as the people we harm.

If my memory serves me correctly, it was Christmas Eve of 1995 when I left home. I was twenty years old, and had a "falling out" with my mother and father. As I said before, my father was a minister. My behavior was expected to be a reflection of the moral life in which I was being taught.

Well, I decided that I no longer wanted to live at home. In fact, I no longer wanted to live a moral life.

So, I set out on my own, my father's "prodigal daughter." During the day, I chased after all the things I was never "allowed" to do when I lived under my parent's roof. Yet, the day would always end. Finally, lying in my bed at night all alone, I would hold a picture of my mother and cry. I would tell my mother all about my day and I would never forget to tell her I loved her and was sorry for not coming home and making things right. Every day, I would go through the same routine. Every night, I would cry myself to sleep, talking to my mother's photograph. She didn't realize the pain I felt as the one causing her such enormous grief. I didn't realize the grief she felt that her "good" daughter had gone astray. Eventually, the picture became weathered and fell apart, but the pain I caused my parents took many years to heal.

There were many persons I had harmed in my addiction: grandparents, aunts, uncles, sisters, nieces, nephews. The pain I caused my parents was the hardest for me to bear in my early recovery. I was sent to numerous psychiatrists and placed on lots of different medications over time, while I was in treatment. Yet, there was no healing. Having my sense of clarity only brought more grief to me, as that meant I had to deal with this pain without being able to numb myself. When God delivered me, He took the greater part of that pain from me. I was able to include in my list many things that were hard for me to think about.

This step is easier said than done. It was very difficult for me to get through. My faith in God was tested during this process. Sometimes, I wanted to go back to feeling "comfortably numb," only to have the revelation occur to me that I would just keep revisiting this pain until I was finally forgiven.

That moment, I told myself, would come some day. I knew that if I kept growing stronger in my recovery the day would come when I would have the opportunity to ask my family's forgiveness. I got through this procedure of doing the eighth step with God's assistance.

During this process, I found it useful to keep a journal. I would jot down things as I would recall them. This was due to the fact that everything I did when I was in my addiction was not perfectly clear to me. A person who is drunk or high doesn't always remember with full clarity everything that was done in an intoxicated state. Sometimes, I would have flashbacks of incidences that I would keep track of in my journal. I watched the movie *21 Days*, starring Sandra Bullock, about a girl going through treatment for an alcohol addiction. She was having dreams at night about drinking and being in bars. She had a lot of flashbacks about the things she did and began to see the peril she was in. I can strongly relate to the character in the movie. I, too, had many dreams and realizations about the somber reality of becoming aware of this devastation.

I kept these thoughts written down in my journal, and throughout this procedure of working step eight, I began to organize my acts of wrongdoing. I made lists of people I had harmed that I could contact, and I also kept a separate list of people I could no longer contact. The important thing was that I was putting it all down on paper. The act of writing these things down releases the soul from bearing the burden, in a sense.

In group therapy, we would practice the act of writing things down on a piece of paper and throwing the paper away. This was relieving, because it sort of freed us from the bondage of the guilt. "*We attempt to sweep away the debris which has accumulated out of our effort to live on self—will and run the show ourselves. If we haven't the will to do this, we ask until it comes. Remember it was agreed at the beginning we would go to any lengths for victory over alcohol.*" (**Alcoholics Anonymous**) p.76. I wrote down all my thoughts "real or imagined" and kept them in my journal. I also looked back on my notes during this time so that I could expand on or clarify my writings of my experiences. Complete honesty is very important in finishing step eight. I had to make sure I didn't leave anything out.

For me, asking forgiveness from others was not always liberating. I think this is actually a very difficult step to follow through. In the first place, who says they'll forgive you? Did my mother and father just open their hearts and say, "Oh, we've been waiting for you to say you were sorry!" No. There was the issue of impulsivity in my addiction. Therefore, my parents forgave me slowly. Over a period of time, and through the very act of remaining sober, their trust in me was reformed. As for my siblings and others, I have faith that our relationship is now pleasant and will improve over time. The hardest thing for them was seeing what I put my parents through. There is not as much personal hurt for the things I did or did not do that they were devastated by. The worst thing to do to someone is to hurt his or her parent(s). I would say that my absence from many important family events caused them much grief, as well.

What if you encounter the situation of asking forgiveness for the things you don't feel bad about? What if you feel justified, and you just don't want to say you're sorry? I've been there. The thing that I have learned to do is control myself. If I'm in a situation that is beyond my control, I must be silent. I may not be able to control the circumstances, but I have to control my tongue to avoid more conflict. This is true for situations at home and in public. Sometimes, it is easier to control your tongue in public than it is to be humble at home, but it will behoove you to follow this point of advice. Even when you know without a doubt that you are right, you are innocent, or you are perfectly sane; you must control yourself. I have had to ask forgiveness for my behavior, when I just defending my rights! Did I enjoy giving someone a piece of my mind? Of course! I enjoyed every "ghetto –fabulous minute of it!" Read Proverbs 15:1 for help.

I have also been in the situation where someone deeply hurt me. I have had to apologize for things I was accused of doing that I didn't do. Trust me, there is a relief in that. When you are trying to heal relationships in your recovery, others will try to keep wedges between you and the ones you are mending fences with. In order to overcome this, you must overcome yourself. Realize who you are and hold on to that. Be humble in your dealings with these people. Remember that they may resent you for changing. When you change, the dynamics in all your relationships change. Some people may like you better as an addict! This gives them more power over you or the situation, in general. Just remember to surrender *everything* to God. "*The moral* inventory *is a cool examination of the damages that occurred to us during life and a sincere effort to look at them in a true perspective. This has the effect of taking the ground glass out of us, the emotional substance that still cuts and inhibits.*" (**As Bill Sees It**) p.140

Chapter Nine: Clean Slate Living

"We are there to sweep off our side of the street, realizing that nothing can be accomplished until we do so..."

Alcoholics Anonymous, pp.77 - 78

Step Nine is about stepping outside of ourselves and considering the feelings of other individuals. We have accomplished recognition of our wrongdoings up to this point in our course. Now, it's time to act. If you have not experienced a soul –cleansing before now, it would be a good time to pray. In Step Nine, we *Made direct amends to such people wherever possible, except when to do so would injure them or others."* What do you think that means? Let me try to explain it to you. Suppose, in your addiction, you found yourself in a compromising situation with the spouse of your best friend. Even supposing nothing really happened, the incident itself happened a long time ago. Would you come forth, years later, to reveal something that could cause devastation in that relationship? As I mentioned in a previous chapter, some things are best left between you and God. Yes, God will forgive you. You will be defeating the purpose of making amends to be so transparent as to try find fellow man's forgiveness for *everything* you ever did wrong to *everyone* you know. Give yourself a break! You must forgive yourself for some things, too. After all, you are trying to create for yourself a clean slate. You're not trying to break the slate!

Having God with me during this time gave me some guidance through this procedure. James 1: 5 reads, "If any of you lacks wisdom, let him ask of God...." I had to get help from God to say what I needed to say in respect and humility. I couldn't just go babbling to everyone I ever hurt and look like a lunatic. I had to use wisdom and discretion in making amends, because I was dealing with other people in pain. There are still some people I have not sought forgiveness from, as well. Don't think that you must go on a road trip to seek out those you think you've harmed. God will begin to present these people to you in situations that are appropriate for the moment. It will be like a "right time and place" kind of situation and God will prick your heart and let you know what to say or do to make the amends. In some cases, God will handle the ordeal where actions, not words, will heal the hurt. In most instances, though, it is best to say, "I'm sorry I hurt you."

I would not suggest ever trying to make amends through the internet or the mail. However, if you find a lost friend on the internet that you need to make amends with, this may be the only way. If possible, plan to meet to make formal apologies. Nobody's perfect. My biggest fear in the publishing of this book is the fear of people coming forth and proclaiming what a terrible person they knew me to be. You simply can't remember everyone. As I mentioned before, there is also the issue of lack of memory due to the intoxication of your brain at that time. There will be those who approach you with things you don't even remember that you did or didn't do. Always keep that humility and think before you speak or do anything.

Making these amends is necessary for your spiritual growth. I know I experienced a rapid spiritual growth once I began making amends with others. Holding on to the past and not making spiritual amends can prevent growth in your recovery. Step Nine moves you into the final healing stages of your recovery process. If you fail to do this, you simply prevent yourself from moving forward in your sobriety. Let go of the past. Say you are sorry, and ask forgiveness whenever possible. Even visiting a grave of someone you never got to say you were sorry to can help you to heal. The person doing the harm suffers the effects of the harm caused. We feel pain, sorrow, loss, just as the ones we hurt feel the same.

Forgiving those who hurt you is part of the healing process, as well. I know people who've held on to grudges for years. This can cause you to be extremely miserable in life. Learn to surrender. Let go of your pain. It is very liberating to know that nothing is holding you back or weighing you down in life. There is freedom in forgiveness. Whether you are asking forgiveness or giving it, it will free you. I don't dwell on my past anymore. I have forgiven my ex –husband and we have been able to move past that place. Would I ever return there? No way! I am not carrying the pain anymore, though. I had nightmares for a year after leaving treatment. God eventually healed my pain, because I was willing to forgive that man.

Just the same, my parents forgave me and the pain was healed for them. How do I know? I know when my mother hugs me and tells me she loves me that she doesn't hurt over me anymore. There is a different sound in her voice, now. The same applies to my father. We have the long conversations we once had together, like he feels comfortable with me again. He is not lecturing me like he was. He's enjoying his time with me when he can.

There is still a slight distance there between my family and my children, but the gap is closing. My wish is that my children will eventually be around their cousins and grandparents much more. I caused the gap during my addiction, but I know that God can fix the mess we make of our lives. We just have to be willing to allow Him to.

Remember that asking forgiveness is not a "one-time deal." We learn to do this through the eighth and ninth steps, but this must be done often. None of us are perfect, so we will continue to make mistakes and hurt others as long as we live. The steps just teach us a new way to live. We must apply these principles every day of our lives to be successful in our sobriety. I have to apologize to my children the most. They see the most vulnerable side of me, knowing me as they do. I like to think we are so close, but I know that I hurt their feelings from time to time. My staying sober helps our relationship to stay strong, but I'm not perfect. I get a lot of practice saying, "I'm sorry. I was wrong." They are learning to be that way, now. I feel that my children are learning to be better people through watching me. They remember the way I was before, and they appreciate my efforts to live a moral, sober lifestyle.

Just staying sober is not enough in recovery. Making these amends will transform your spiritual defects and replace them with attributes. Helping others is also important in this process. Sharing our testimonies helps others see what they may need to change. If you don't go to meetings, you may find support in church. I believe that fellowship keeps us encouraged and directed towards total healing of addiction. I have been to meetings and church, and I always enjoyed both. It feels good to give someone words of encouragement. It feels just as good to get those words of encouragement when I need them.

Constant humility is necessary in recovery. Ask for forgiveness. Give forgiveness. Help others to see that forgiveness heals pain. Keep doing this, because Step Nine never ends.

Chapter Ten: Daily Commitment

"Continued to take personal inventory and when we were wrong promptly admitted it."

The Twelve Steps of Alcoholics Anonymous

Step ten is a continuation of step nine. Step nine helped me to learn to say, "I'm sorry." Step ten is just a daily act of this. This is a good place to mention keeping a daily devotional. In a daily devotional, you are led by the scriptures through topics. This will help you see things you need to continue to change in yourself; not just saying I'm sorry.

As I evolved into a new person, I had to change many things about myself along the way.

I thought differently, therefore, I dressed differently and behaved differently. As a result of these changes taking place in my mind and spirit, saying I made a mistake became easier.

I mentioned before that I did not work the twelve steps alone. I also used other materials to enhance my experience of spiritual growth. There are many self-help books and a wide array of topics. Foremost, I would recommend reading the Bible. Some people, though, are also recovering from a lifetime of baggage. Childhood abuse, sexual or physical, must be devastating to overcome. I listened to many cases while in treatment. The girls that I became associated with in the treatment center had overcome such horrible conditions to get to the places they were in their recoveries. I had to admire them for even being there. Some of them had been traded for drugs as children by their fathers and/or mothers. One had been passed between her fathers friends from the time she was two-years-old. How do you overcome such a devastatingly horrible childhood?

Then, when you live the way you were taught to live, you are punished for it.

This is why I mention the self–help books. If you are trying to overcome cancer, you buy books about surviving cancer. There are even books on surviving the loss of a child. What causes addiction, and how do you survive this devastating affliction? I found materials on building character in children, changing attitude problems, even being a better homemaker. All these materials were useful to me in my recovery. As I mentioned, I was twenty years old when I began to drink heavily. The things I should have been learning to prepare myself for being a wife and mother were not in my thoughts at that time. I missed key opportunities for these experiences that would've prepared me for this, because I was not in a state of clarity to retain any useful information at that stage in my life. The greatest resource for me now is the Bible. The book of Proverbs is a great place to start. It's easy to understand and is like a little instruction book for life.

Step ten instructs us to keep a daily self–inventory. *"For the wise have always known that no one can make much of his life until self–searching becomes a regular habit, until he is able to admit and accept what he finds, and until he patiently and persistently tries to correct what is wrong."* (**Twelve Steps and Twelve Traditions**) p. 88. For me, some days are better than others. In keeping my personal inventory, I am able to see that my circumstances are not the problem. I am the problem. I have been able to retrain myself to respond more consistently to problems, because I realize that I respond based on my own spiritual state at the time.

Once we begin keeping our own records of personal defects and victories, we'll be able to have more victories than defects, thus, being constantly aware of behavior characteristics helps to reform the negative behavior that is otherwise known as "addictive behavior." Remember that each step takes time. We don't change overnight. Working the steps is a progression into a new way of life. If you are willing to take these steps toward spiritual change, you will eventually begin to reap the benefits of living a rewarding life.

Begin keeping a moral inventory every day, or keep your original self –inventory, simply adding daily thoughts as you go along. Keep in mind that if you were fighting to beat any other ailment, you would do whatever it would take to preserve or prolong your life. I looked at doing all this work as fighting to beat a terminal illness. This disease is terminal. It is fatal. Romans 6:23 reads, *"For the wages of sin is death, but the gift of God is eternal life in Christ Jesus our Lord."* This *is* a terminal condition. You *will* die if you don't recover.

"Continue to watch for selfishness, dishonesty, resentment, and fear. When these crop up, we ask God at once to remove them…" (**Alcoholics Anonymous**) p. 84. I have more compassion for others when I stay in a constant state of humility. Serving others before myself was once difficult for me. If someone upset me, I'd act rashly, and then hold a grudge forever. That behavior is debilitating! Keeping a daily inventory helps to change that behavior. I no longer run away from my problems, moving my children from place to place. I have managed to stabilize their lives by keeping my thoughts and behaviors in constant check.

I always try to remember that God delivered me from this addiction so that I could give the credit back to Him. Psalm 40:1-3 reads, *"I waited patiently for the Lord; and He inclined to me, and heard my cry. He also brought me up out of a horrible pit, out of the miry clay, and set my feet on a rock, and established my steps. He has put a new song in my mouth –Praise to our God; many will see it and fear, and will trust in the Lord."* I believe that God saves us for His very name's sake. In other words, what kind of God would He be if He let us die like this? It is for the sake of all who see His magnificent works to know that He is such an awesome God. My life is lived for the glory of God, as a testimony to His greatness. He has put a new song in my mouth! I now sing, "Look what my God can do!"

The reason it is so important to keep this daily inventory and watch my behavior is so that I can spread the message, helping others by living a sober lifestyle. I want to be an example of living a successful, sober life. It takes effort to stay on the wagon. By doing the self –inventories, I can keep track of my own progress. I am grateful to be sober every day that I wake up. I have a picture hanging over my bed that reads, "Each new day is a gift… That's why we call it *'the present'*."

I can assure you of this: As time goes on in your recovery process, you will think of drinking and/or using less and less if you do what you are supposed to do to stay sober. When I first entered treatment, I woke up sweating and looking for any kind of "fix" I could have gotten. I never got it, so I got better. When I quit smoking, I would time myself further and further apart on cigarettes, until I finally didn't think I'd die if I didn't have one. Eventually, I didn't think of drinking anymore at all. So, when doing self –inventories, I also kept track of cravings. I noticed the decline in the cravings and the eventual "no cravings today." Some people don't think this is possible. I believe that God took the desire from me. That would be the secret to my success as a recovering addict. If you desire something, work hard for it. God will give you wisdom and power to overcome any addiction. Whether it is sex, drugs, gambling, or just smoking and/or drinking; God is able to help you overcome. Here is your hope: He will empower you with strength from His High Place.

Keep record of your strengths, weaknesses, accomplishments, and failures so that you can see your growth. It will encourage you during this step to do that. If you are like me, you will be amazed at your own progress.

Chapter Eleven: Centered

"But first of all we shall want sunlight; nothing much can grow in the dark.
Meditation is our step out into the sun."
As Bill Sees It, p.10

In working the Eleventh Step, I began to come out of the shadows of my addiction. By trading my "stinking thinking" for new ideas, I was able to perceive why I was incapable of sustaining healthy relationships with others. Many problems I had to contend with throughout my addiction were caused by my poor choices and ailing lifestyle. There was no dark cloud above my head. I had been creating messes for myself! The eleventh step is simple, *"Sought through prayer and meditation to improve our conscious contact with God, as we understood Him, praying only for knowledge of His will for us and the power to carry that out."* Theoretically, I'm to first learn how to pray to God (conscious contact). Then, I'm to stay focused on His will for *me* (praying only for *knowledge* of His will). Finally, I am to ask Him for help to complete His will (the *power* to carry that out). So, this is what I pray, "God, thank you for this day of sobriety and serenity. Demonstrate Your will for me today. Help me to remain centered on myself, which will keep me out of trouble. You know I am unable to resolve my problems, so help me stay out of others' problems today. Keep me safe from deception, so that I will not fall into the hand of this addiction today. Empower me with Your divine purpose for me today. Amen." He will show me His will as we go along if I keep a conscious contact with Him throughout the day. This must be done *every* day.

When we learn to listen for God's instruction, we can be of some use to others still besieged by addiction. If we do not seek God, we can't help others, because we are powerless to stay buoyant ourselves. A friend of mine recently gave me this analogy of being stuck in addiction, "It must feel like you are stuck out on a big lake in a boat with no paddles, no motor, no life jackets, and no radio to call for help. You can see the shore, but no one can hear you calling for help. You would have to call on God. He'd be your only choice!" I thought that was a pretty insightful analogy, coming from a friend who didn't smoke or drink.

Until I reached a certain point in my own recovery, it didn't even occur to me to write this book. As God began to bring about certain changes in my life, I desired to share my story with others. Once I improved my conscious contact with Him, I realized that was His will. If I had been diagnosed with a terminal illness and found a miracle cure, I would share that with the whole world. I would *everyone* to have access to the cure and receive treatment, if needed. I would hope that even a family member of someone afflicted with the disease would find my cure and deliver it to the ill. This is my hope for those afflicted with the illness of addiction. The cure is God. The process of finding God came through the step work, for me. I was indifferent to the word of God, after hearing so many sermons as a child. My life was spent in church. It didn't faze me to sit in church. God managed to break through my barriers of stone to reach me.

My bottom was the moment I stood on my bed with that bedpost in my hands. I was done. I embraced recovery like a child with a new toy. Once I achieved the position in my development to work Step Eleven, I had already surrendered to God. He was able to communicate His will to me, because I was in the palm of His hand. When we surrender to God, He owns us, including our will. We are like clay in His hand. He begins to mold us. Isaiah 64:8 reads, *"But now, O Lord, You are our Father; We are the clay, and You our potter; and all we are the work of Your hand."* Communication with God keeps me sober. Things must go according to His will, not mine. When things were done my way, my life was a mess. Constant meditation on God keeps my will under His authority.

Some people have a hard time being under submission to anything or anyone. However, under our own authority we lack the ability to manipulate our environment to properly function, thus creating a dysfunctional life. This would be considered a spiritual barrier if we made no conscious contact with God. For those who don't like to pray, *"Almost the only scoffers at prayer are those who never tried it enough."* (**Twelve Steps and Twelve Traditions**) p. 97. Prayer brings about change in our lives, whether we believe or not. My husband is not the type to loudly proclaim the marvelous works of God in his life. Supplication is not a topic he discusses openly. However, before our trip to the beach last year, he prayed for God to let it rain while we were there. He prayed that prayer just to see if god would answer it. It rained the first three days we were there, so he told me about the dream. I believe God answered his prayer to increase his faith. If you don't know how to pray, that's okay. The more often you pray, the more you begin to see changes take place in your life.

If the steps are worked correctly, you will realize that you are seeing these changes take place in your life before realizing that you are changing. Other people will begin to tell you they detect the changes in you long before you detect them in yourself. I don't regret surrendering my will to God. My husband and I tell each other quite often that it is a good feeling to be sober. There is a peace in knowing that you don't have anything to feel guilty about when you go to bed at night. If you do your moral inventory and spend time in prayer and meditation each day, you will begin to feel the serenity of being sober.

Chapter Twelve: Not Just About Me

"Having had a spiritual awakening as a result of these steps, we tried to carry this message to alcoholics and to practice these principles in all our affairs."
Twelve Steps and Twelve Traditions, p. 106

My spiritual awakening happened that day I was offered a beer by my boss. When that small voice inside of so profoundly let me know who was at the wheel in my life, I suddenly realized that I wasn't doing this by myself. Only by the power of God was I able to go without drinking. I didn't desire to be drunk, either. To remain sober, we must change from the attitude of desiring intoxication to the attitude of desiring clarity of mind. We no longer are self—seeking, but have a desire to please others.

Since I have been in recovery, I have grown spiritually. I know that I still have a long way to go, but I made a few milestones that I can be proud of, as well. I am now active in church, and I volunteer at the same treatment center I once sought help from. I feel it a duty and an honor to be able to help others. My desire is to one day be able to meet the One, face-to-face, who washed me white as snow and set my feet on a new path. The other night I had a dream that I went up in the Rapture. I dreamt that, as I felt my body come up off the ground, my voice began to change. When I tried to speak, I had already taken on a heavenly voice not of this earth. I woke up feeling the very meaning of the word *splendor*. The scripture that was on my mind when I awakened was Luke 12:34,"For where your treasure is, there your heart will be also."

Since I have been in recovery, I have met many people whose lives have been affected by addiction. I have met those trapped in the snares of their own addictions. I have even met people who are raising the children of addicts not ready to let go of this affliction. I feel there has been a divine purpose in my having met these people. I hope that my testimony of triumph over this disease can help others either find their own way, or help a loved one find his or her way out of the darkness. My own soul is at peace, knowing that I've overcome my own demons. Yet, I cannot be satisfied with that alone. I don't think God set me free to no purpose. There is a purpose in everything great that God does. I hope that I have sincerely and obediently followed his will in writing this book, and that everything I shared can be for the Glory of God. If I make no other substantial points in this memoir, I want it to be understood that I got here through the grace and delivering power of God.

Once I had my spiritual awakening, I realized right away that I had to go and share my story with others so they could have what I have. Sobriety is a wonderful state of living, and the serenity of sober living is a wonderful and priceless gift to have. If I continue to follow the way of Christ, I will continue to live a peaceful life on Earth and join my deliverer for eternal peace and serenity in Heaven.

I am reminded of another scripture in the Bible, found in Micah 6:8,"*He has shown you, O man, what is good; and what does the Lord require of you but to do justly, to love mercy, and to walk humbly with your God?*" I think all God really wants us to do is make that daily effort to seek Him. For those of us in recovery, it is necessary for survival. I don't think with the mindset that I may relapse tomorrow, for there is no hope in that way of thinking. Every day, I must keep my mind focused on staying sober. I cannot help others unless I have this attitude.

Each of the steps is a procedure that produces the result of spiritual growth. Many consumers in treatment facilities are indifferent towards the twelve steps and towards AA, as a program. The experience taught me that until I was ready to "take certain steps" I would not recover. I understand how it feels to enjoy addiction. I thought I was having a good time when I was drunk or high. Before I had children, I didn't realize I was an alcoholic. I had a good time every night of the week, chasing life. I had to suffer to get to the place in my life where recovery was what I knew I needed.

They say every person has to hit bottom. My bottom was the dark hell of domestic violence. It wasn't fun anymore to be alive. I would rather have been dead than alive back then. I lived for the sake of my children. I now realize my children don't have the power to save me from myself. Only God can fill the hole inside of me that addiction only enlarged. I once hated my life so much that I needed to be numb to live it. I remember waking up every morning disappointed to have made it through another night. I wondered what purpose there was in my being alive. Not too long ago, I heard a sermon about god's purpose for each of us. The preacher said, "Our only purpose in Life is to glorify God, our creator. That's all he made us for." That seemed simple to me. I am writing my memoir to glorify my creator. For others to know that Christ is the cure for any affliction is my purpose in writing this book.

If you are enabling an addict, stop. Don't help him or her anymore. You will only see change when the person you are trying to help has to suffer. We just don't ask for help until we are broken down. It is hard to allow those we love to hit bottom. We don't want to see them hurting. I declare to you as a recovering addict that it necessary to do this. If you will let go, God will take over. *"The sacrifices of God are a broken spirit: a broken and a contrite heart, O God, thou wilt not despise."* Psalm 51:17. I suffered in great agony until I saw a light in my darkness. I knew that living sober had to be better than living in addiction. I accepted, graciously, the lifeline that was thrown to me.

My story is the story of a miracle. The miracle is that the person I once was no longer exists. I have evolved into a new being who doesn't even resemble the one who was an addict. Today, I am a devoted mother who adores my children. I breathe clean air into my lungs, and it feels good. I can feel the oxygen refresh my veins. Like the woman at the well, I was once a shell of a person. I found the living water, and I can feel it coursing through me, sustaining me. I can stay sober today, because there was no substance for me in substances. Only God can fill that emptiness. Today, I am sober. Today, I am validated. Today, I have a purpose. Today, I am centered.

www.ingramcontent.com/pod-product-compliance
Lightning Source LLC
Chambersburg PA
CBHW020410290526
45785CB00005B/2499